Chapter 1

I am not my own limitation, but in my past years I would sit and pout to a listening ear about what I ignorantly had discerned as my own failures in my course of this life. Today, I ponder on my successes, but most importantly I notice how beautiful it is to be limitless and financially free. Being true to yourself and overcoming worries, criticisms, fears, and doubts from global masses and my own ego are just some of the ideals that many college students, including myself, had to learn to adapt to before mid-sophomore year. It is not only after you have done your requirements to graduate a community college, but when you first get to engage in a community college that you learn that your past does not depict your future and you begin to grow and learn accordingly and not look at your shortcomings in any subject as a failure.

When it comes to stabilizing a college life with your future having financial support there is often a struggle to you as a parent, student, or even a professor to really grasp your vision because of lack, need, and the bills that you have created. You must trust in yourself that you successfully made the correct moves to stabilize harmony and prosperity in your life despite any of the negatives. You must trust yourself completely and fully with or without completing a college life. You are not a victim of life and its situations you are a success and your direct choices in your life have led you to view this book on my focus and the law of attraction.

We are all limitless creators of our own reality. I learned how powerful our minds are and how limitless our imagination evolves into our internal reality when I stopped depicting myself as a limitation or problem but began to think of my realities as projects. Viewing my problems as projects have allowed me to focus on solutions to my problems and allow non-resistant energy to flow with the never sleeping law of attraction. Functioning in my way of looking at the circumstances of my reality as a project rather than a problem aided to my motivation for change which was activated and increased immensely. The more that you are motivated the more you begin to remember more of what you have learned about your task or life, and you will more than often succeed in your projects, but you must also know that it is very imperative to welcome the lessons that the project presents and accept them with love, learning and growing from the project's lessons.

It is known by many generational scholars and elders that if you accept the lessons of life as gifts "projects" to learn from and stay steady in growing from in a healthy way then life will continue to give you the gift's "projects" you desire to learn and grow from in a healthy way. The healthy way that life will present these gifts or opportunities to you will aid you in your success. Many have a rags to riches story and so do I, one that starts with me growing up in a desolate wilderness area sharecropping in the Ozark Moutain area of Arkansas. It continues with me being subject to a gang life, and a drug abusive life in the Midwest of America, but overall, I was looking for my gift's in life in all the wrong places instead of focusing on my own positive aspects of intuition and love allowing loving opportunities to present themselves to me.

Seemingly in my trial and error stages, by the age of 17 years old I had a list of misdemeanors and felonies that included 2 class B felonies dealing in cocaine and a brain aneurysm due to what the doctors deemed was caused from stress.

My ignorance of not knowing that the gentrification in society and the social gas lighting from you peers will cause you to see and believe in limits that will bind you against your right of good sense of opinion and choice, making some people seem to be envious towards you while you intentionally hate others for their right doings towards you perceiving them to be wrongful by the neglect of your own proper interpretation. I believe that there are limitless possibilities for me and everyone that is reading this book. I believe that are limitless possibilities to be sought out during each second that we breathe during this life. There are 60 seconds to a minute, and 60 minutes to an hour which means that in a year you have 525,600 possibilities to make the positive choice in acting on an idea.

If you were to count how many choices per day that we humans make per our thoughts from yesterday's opportunities, you will see that we have 500,000+ opportunities of choices to choose from deriving from our thoughts and desires each year. Out of many opportunities we can choose from per year there, are some life altering opportunities for long-term life changes waiting for acceptance and approval. Maybe you had the opportunity to marry the love of your life, or maybe you had the opportunity to start a good job with benefits, or even you had made the choice of opportunity to start your own business. Whatever the case in your situation is, you will see how you had found your power to make the conscious decision to say yes to an opportunity. Your past is your conviction and your conviction should be a gift in the opportunities in your life that will aid you in motivated and massive growth.

Be aware of saying no to a positive opportunity because it is the same as being your own negative limitation. Your positive actions of positive choices will always speak louder than the words and voices of ignorance. Our planet Earth always vibrates in accordance with the vibrations you constantly live by. When your thoughts, feelings, or actions are positive or negative the law of attraction engages in a process of calibration in accordance with your vibrations which are governed by the law and the universal laws of our planet Earth.

Your choice of the opportunities that present themselves to you is in your focus. When you have an idea begin to take a planned action on the idea and the opportunity presented from the idea is then will be read and available to be formed into your goal. Begin focusing on your goal as it is already completed within the realms of you mind as little or as much as life will allow you in your present moment of circumstantial thought. I firmly believe that proper preparation prevents poor performance in your desired focus.

Allow your new plan to be planted in your mental garden to be nurtured and groomed as if you are a farmer tending to his best crop yet. Remember the fact that nothing is to small an idea or to grandeur a dream. Small seeds grow into mighty oaks with the love and care. Nurture your ideas it to fruition as the Earth gives us its gift of love and life.

If you have encountered a past instance of poverty know that it does not warrant any personal provisions of notice for you to give up on your dreams. If you must accommodate your goal by taking baby steps to see it being fulfilled, it is best to do so with fearless confidence keeping the end result of the success you wish in mind. Know that by just making the decision to take the baby steps necessary that it is a justification that you struck gold on your road to engaging in your success. You will then see your seedling grow into a producing tree the fruits of your labor and be rewarded by and enjoyed with your harvest which when harvested will be replanted for a future harvest.

The effort you take to initiate action on your idea will speak the successes of perseverance, endurance, and riches. The effort that you take towards success will entail your worth of wealth and self-efficacy found within yourself. The growth and development in the action of focusing that you show will be received by the vibrations of your actions from the law of attraction and then gifted to you in plenty by both the law of attraction and the universal law of Focus. The universal law of Focus interprets how what you focus on grows.

You are a victor which separates you from the negative damaging energies of doubt and worry hindering your progression towards the completion of your projects. When the energies of doubt and worry come to visit you before you make the decision to start the journey to complete your desired goals, they will hold an intense of persuasion over you. Stay focused on your projected planned project. If you stay focused on a planned project, by you it will then become a complete goal.

For you the reader, focusing and understanding my writing this far, I am truly proud of you and would like to invite you to enjoy this book's profound teachings until the end page. Also please do not misinterpret me when I speak of the low-income families, college struggles, or any formidable circumstance. I do not expect many to resonate with any past circumstance, but the correlation between positive and negative reactions caused by focus and the law of attraction are very prudent to be realized. Poverty is innocuous when you have focus on a goal and execute even if it takes extreme will power the law of attraction will bring back to you gifts of opportunity and success.

An intelligent woman who used an extreme amount of will power to honor her dream by connecting her goals is Lisa Nichols, a now motivational speaker, author, and multi-million dollar business owner who, as I, understood intense focus and while growing up, living, and learning in the rolling 60's error in Los Angeles, Ca.

Lisa Nichols talked about being a victim of her environment which brought her to leading a life of being a single mother, tenacious in her desire to fulfill her dreams all while having had saved for

3 years to plant her major seed of desire that she now lives under many of extenuating circumstances. Giving up was not an option for her, I, and millions of other individuals that came from impoverished environments in the United States of America. Unlike her story which had begun in Los, Angeles, California during the 1960's more of my story begin in the 1980's in my small birth town of Michigan City, Indiana. Through court cases of custody between my mother and father and the hardships of being misunderstood had led me to the juvenile system that soon after became the jail system.

Being broke and broke down mentally and emotionally seemed impossible to repair without immense and intense focus, the law of attraction, and a sense of a higher power of energy. My intentions of wring this book are to not only inform readers about the power of focus and the law of attraction, but to place emphasis on placing a goal together with a desired plan of action. I want to inform readers on having belief in themselves and faith that the universal law of attraction always works to aid you. In between many moments in my young life I never gave up on my desire to live the life of a bestselling author and graduate college because of my focus and belief in myself and faith in the law of attraction.

Drug abuse and gang life was pivotal in my teenage my stage of my reality, but with my goals being backed with a desire to thrive I seen many successes some big and some small. In my success I found it less stressful to take many baby steps that had accompanied my focus and my live vibration to calibrate with the law of attraction. I noticeably to many found a faith, belief, and love in myself to succeed. God wants us all to succeed so as we were born with a magical part of him called imagination which no animal, insect, or plant on this planet has.

When you channel in focus you allow your imagination to fill in the blanks with your truth and in your imagination, there is no sense of poverty. In your imagination there are only your visions and what it feels like for you to have your visions become wishes fulfilled. Although obtaining you goal projects require action from you, envision the as already having been complete and the law of attraction will deliver to you more of the feeling of being complete. If you have moments of doubt and worry, as quickly as those thoughts can enter your mind, they will give caution to the law of attraction, but they can be removed as soon as you change your thoughts as they enter your mind.

To focus on maintaining a happy and healthy mind, body, and soul does not want any thoughts or feelings of doubt, worry, or stresses. To have a focus means to be in the state of focus or have quality of having or producing a clear visual definition to focus on. When you use your imagination to focus on your goal it is of importance for you to also envision the mental feelings of seeing yourself completing your goal or seeing your goal as being completed by you. You must have faith in your own self and believe in the empowering moments of opportunity you will encounter along the way to reaching your end goal.

How to focus with intent, faith, and belief in yourself is a very admirable philosophy taught by Andrew Carnegie to Napoleon Hill and learned by millions of humans including Bob Proctor and myself. This is more than a philosophy, but a proven fact that saved not only my direction of life, but Bob Proctor and millions of others life direction. This study of truth shows and tells the power of your mind when you focus. As in the Law of Attraction your thoughts create the actions you focus on.

It is very imperative to believe in yourself and goals and that you protect your goals starting when they are your given gifts of thought in your imagination. Thoughts become things is the a very simplified reason of magnetism concerning the Law of Attraction. Know that no one can make you believe in yourself or your goals but yourself. Know that this is not a race, but a quest you must do on your own; with trust and in believing in yourself and in the words of this prayer known as the serenity prayer by the alcoholics anonymous groups:

God grant me the serenity to accept the things I cannot change, courage to change the things I can, and wisdom to know the difference.

Earlier, I had stated that I had noticed myself as being my own limitation. I felt that is had been my own limitation since I was ignorant to the fact that life was happening for me and not too me. I was my own limitation by me constantly finding short-term solutions to long-term situations. Although I had planted my seed in my mind to fulfill my end goal, the feelings of doubt, worry, and poverty had made it difficult for me to connect with the feelings of having a wish fulfilled or being a success until I grew older. Being able to connect with me as the successful man I am was a battle in teenage and my young adult years until age 35.

Sometimes we must lose the battle to win the war. In Greek mythology King Pyrrhus of Epirus, defeated the Romans at Asculum in a.d. 279, but lost his best officers and many of his troops and when he stated, "Another such victory and **we** are lost." King Pyrrhus chose to see the battle for what it was in his eyes which was a win. He had known then that if he had had lost the battle, he would have had the opportunity to win the war.

Staying and keeping focus requires battles to be overcome, but you will win the war so stay the course. It is always best to keep your mind over the long-term solutions in your life to help nurture your goal to success without stumbling to a halt over short-term problems. When you choose to take the gift of an opportunity to create your goals completion with a confident desire you are also choosing to learn from the loses, some are minimal, you encounter along your way to success.

Chapter 2

Focusing requires an attentive desire with affirmative action towards the goal you choose to focus on. It was Abraham Hicks who had gave an explanation on the law of attraction and stated that it is important to know of what you do not want in your life, but you must not focus on that which you do not want. When we focus too much on what we do not want, we start to create limiting beliefs within ourselves. These beliefs are roadblocks to our prosperity consciousness. In my life I have noticed the fact that what I had focused on gained momentum and grew in substantial ways.

The power of focus orchestrates beautifully with the law of attraction. Just as the law of attraction expresses how like attracts to your likeness of your desire. By focusing on what you desire you soon adopt a plan and the what you desire becomes what you focus your attention on while following your plan to complete the goal. By the law of focus and the law of attraction being in harmony with each other having a sound plan to complete goals is almost definite, but possible.

When we understand how to focus and how what we give action to the ideas that we focus on we will automatically notice growth. In planning alone is the desired result of growth. Having a focus allows us to understand how well these 2 laws, The Law of Attraction and The Law of Focus, work in accordance with or goals completion and also for the betterment of our lives. These 2 laws work in a harmonious way to prevent any event of failure and failure is when you fail to complete a goal only to stop your focus which will stop the Law of Attraction.

What lies within each human is their true purpose. In order to reveal your true purpose, you must remove yourself from feelings of doubt as if your desires are not attainable and worry by feelings of depression by you just focusing on the things that provide you financial bliss and inner peace and happiness. There may be times that you will have to alter the plans you have due to short-term upheavals but keep your goals in place for the long-term successful completion of your goal. It is always best to agree to disagree while you live your life on life's terms.

To better focus you must overcome any fears that cause you a lack of focus. Remember that one of the ways that the law of attraction works is to attract to you what we do not want in our lives by giving it focus. Do not give focus to wants, needs, or lacks. I will list to you 6 ways that increase your focus and describe them clearly and in an understanding way.

1. Focus on one thing at a time.

When you focus on one thing at a time you mainstream your attention to the task at hand looking forward to success. Breaking a goal down to focus on simple plans will alleviate you of any fears that stop you from completing your goal.

2. Keep good health, some type of physical and mental workout plan and stay full of positive energy.

I love to read daily, mediate daily, go for walks, or jog daily which are just some ways to stay healthy, physically fit, mentally fit, and increase positive actions and activity. Staying fit in many areas pertaining to your mind and the body will decrease any fears of warranted ill health both within and in the surrounding world including procrastinating symptoms of, sleepiness, tiredness, and lack of enthusiasm.

3. Have clear developed and defined goals that are in line with your vision and true intention.

When you have clearly developed defined goals, you can act on your goals with intent and determination. You are then able to focus your full attention on your goals. With your increased focus you will also notice the new level of emotional security you continue to keep.

4. You must have faith in yourself and in your abilities.

When you take time to focus on your own thoughts, ideas, or goals those entities you gave your attention and action too begin to take on life. There is a quote in the chapter of Hebrews in the holy bible that says that:

Hebrews 11:1-6 King James Version (KJV)

11 *Now faith is the substance of things hoped for, the evidence of things not seen.*

5. You must realize that "all" distractions are equal and when you give attention to them, they become counterproductive.

Stay focused on your vision. Do not allow anything person, irrelevant situation, thought, or form of criticism to disturb you in completing your goal. During our human lives we all have distractions, but it is the choices that you make along your path that will discern if the distractions are short or long lived.

6. Control your body, instincts, and emotions.

I was reading a book by Dr. Herbert Harris and the universal law of focus was discussed by him in more depth and detail. In the book he reasons that in controlling your body, instincts, and emotions you must take a keen possession of your mind. Your thoughts create your actions which take the form of your bodily instincts, attitude, self-image of yourself, and a positive or a negative focus. Your self image is by design the person you deeply know that you are, and even when your current reality does not match your self image your self image will always be the truth of who you are as a person.

I have come to embrace my self image through many adversaries. I have come to love my true self and be loved from myself and others. The reason the self image you have within yourself happens many times during your childhood is because your focus is on peer pressures, but your personality always shows. You would never once thought to think that the growth and developmental stages of your life can be innocuous, but sometimes they are.

In my case it has been always fear, doubt, worry and for myself and many of you were the 3 major negative hinderances too my focus. It is true that somethings start during childhood, but they have a lasting imprint throughout your life's quest. To some the 3 hinderances of thier focus is sibling chatter or the criticism from friends and family. I have 5 real sisters, 3 brothers from different social environments and criticism from them placed doubt, worry, and fear of them , sometimes, but ultimately fear of my success in me.

During one occasion I often have nostalgia about was the moment I had gotten certified in Human Potential. There I was elated about how I was being welcomed and had succeeded with distant friends to receive an award when my phone, which was on vibrate, began vibrating wildly 63 times. I know it was 63 times because one of my mentors and I counted the messages each time. It was at the 63rd time, the messages between them came fast when they could have just called each other, my phone vibrated and my mentor and others gave me a look of caution that was felt so I had told my him and others how my siblings and my biological mother were often chatting around me and showed him my phone, but allowing love and communication to live he suggested to me to write a letter to them about how I feel and to this very day I have got no response to the letter from them, but he knew it was more of how I felt in that moment and in the future to focus during both times.

Once again, I was doing my final task in being certified in Human potential which has a tremendous amount to do with emotional intelligence. If you allow any avoidance, doubt, lack, or criticism to enter your mind space it will destroy your dream. I was hurt, he saw it, and knew them and a letter to them did not hold weight in their minds, but was coachable and did as suggested to me by my mentor texting a 3-page text letter to them about how I felt for years, where I was during that moment, and how I loved them all. Instantly I felt a rush of relief and openly gave myself praise for taking such a step with confidence and not fear.

Although the chatter between them continued to go on from the group chat between them they never once texted me back or making a comment about my text or tried to call me which had my mentor furious at them, but calm with me. He then directed me to just cut my phone off for the duration of time for my health and focus and to ignore them for a time to come for the same reasons. That was some great coaching advice because you must learn to find love and understanding in yourself when you cannot feel or receive it from anyone else family included. To stay focused you must focus more on your end goal than on your surroundings even during the situations and the times that it hurts. Living and loving a joyous life requires focus and your focus includes you to controlling your actions, discerning your thoughts, discern words which can impact thoughts, and to make positive decisions of choice in all your activities.

I personally have had many moments that required my choice of how to engage in focus including holidays, family functions, class assignments in college, father duties, and work obligations where I had to remain focused on the various tasks. One of the best ways to stay focused that I still use to this day is keeping a calendar of my days and writing down my plan to reach my goals. Each morning after I wake and meditate, I view my calendar which includes my plans and my goal list. My calendar keeps me on a positive and steady track of my daily activities. I also journal each day to set the stage of my own positive thoughts and the positive intentions I decide to explore more of each day.

If you can think the thought in your mind, you can feel it in your mind to the same as some dreams feel real. It is a fact that if you can think your goals and feel them it in your mind, then they are worth adding emotion and the deserved ingredient of focus to bring them to life.

Chapter 3

The best way to focus is to supplant the thoughts and feelings in your subconscious mind that you

desire to focus on. "Focus on where you want to go, not on what you fear." — Tony Robbins.

Conscious focus is led by your human magnetism or ego daily and even times while we sleep during the R.E.M. process. During the process of R.E.M. sleep your subconscious mind takes focus of the characters that are orchestrated in your mind while you dream.

The subconscious mind makes the expansion of your focus easier both while you are dreaming and while you are awake. According to the universal law of attraction your subconscious mind works with your conscious mind to emit the exact same frequency of the entity you desire or focus on. What you focus on will exponentially grow with the required focus and the law of attraction working in accordance with each other. The (yen) or conscious and the (yang) or subconscious sections of the mental muscle, your brain, require an overall feeling, and when you focus on your desired goal by seeing through your goal form from start to the finish, the feeling you will have is a positive and joyous feeling of having a wish being fulfilled.

The feeling from your positive focus will then take president in your mind gaining the attention of the structured Universal Law of Attraction. The Universal Law of Attraction is always working. The Law of Attraction works is a natural universal law and works with the emotions and feelings you gain from focus. Therefore, the Law of Attraction will attract to us those things we either like or do not like in alignment with the emotional vibrations and frequency we admit when we focus on either essential working tasks, writing a song to standard, writing a book to completion, focusing on problems, worries, complaints, or arguments.

Whatever or whoever the person or the circumstance that you confide in the Law of Attraction will not be prejudice about delivering the exact results back to you that you felt in that precise moment. The simple, but harsh truth we all have to face is not only that when you know better you do better, but the fact is that we are all the root cause to our own problems each day by the equivalent emissions of frequency from our thoughts throughout our lives. Can the decision to make your thoughts be positive or negative thoughts, the choice is yours. When you focus you act in emotion and feeling, and the Law of Attraction reads and responds to your controlled or uncontrolled actions of feelings.

 According to the Law of Attraction any condition is perfect for it to correspond to the nature of our most dominant thoughts in our conscious and subconscious mind. Any habitual thought pattern and belief in our conscious mind are always being communicated to the universal Law of Attraction, so it is wise to keep your thoughts positive. The Universal Law of Attraction responds and realizes every area of our life including our health relationship with our inner and outer body, our finances in and out of our bank account, and all our family and love relationships. Keep your thoughts positive and notice how what you focus on grows because the Law of Attraction gives you back more of the thing that has you emotionally acting on an action and feeling.

A great thing about the Universal Law of Attraction is how it can always be intensified by using emotions and desired focus. The Universal Law of Attraction works just as great for the non-religious as it does for the religious, even though in some religions it is controversial to their religious beliefs, but religions acknowledge key components that make the Law of Attraction work which are focus, thoughts, feeling, and action and those requirements equal a simple equation without any religious tendencies. Simply put, if you can think it, you can focus on it, you can act on it, you can feel it as you act on it. The reality of how the Law of Attraction works is that it requires the use of both your conscious mind and subconscious mind to work in harmony using your emotional thoughts, the value of your feelings, and your desired actions.

For religious concerns there is a very informative and reputable understanding of the Universal Law of Attraction asserted in a biblical quote that I have had the liberty to correlate with certainty. The quote is a scripture from the holy bible addressing the Law of Attraction's divine likeness: Phillipians 4:8 that concludes...

"Finally, brethren, whatsoever things are true, whatsoever things are honest, whatsoever things are just, whatsoever things are pure, whatsoever things are lovely, whatsoever things are of good report; if there be any virtue, and if there be any praise, think on these things." – Philipians 4:8

Another biblical quote which gives reference to the existing Universal Law of Attraction is:

"As a man thinks, so is he." – Proverbs 23:7

In many religions there is a major focus on the scriptures of the holy bible, and what conspires with the connection to religious focus in accordance with the universal Law of Attraction. The above scriptures imply to you that what you perceive to be true is true and to what you focus on is of praise. It goes on to imply the fact to keep your thoughts, actions, and ideas positive. Your thoughts form into existing things and will attract to them more thoughts and more existing things that are in the same form and connection as your prior positive thoughts or your negative thoughts.

Focusing on your thoughts, bringing action to your goals, and the Universal Law of Attraction all work in harmony with one another. It is my goal to make sure that you get a grasp on this connection before I move on to deeper waters of our living knowledge and truth about this subject. Have you ever had an idea from that of a ponder or a dream you've had, made a definite plan for it, put the plan into your desired action to complete the designated goal, and completed your goals achievement? When you use the sensory system in your mind which god has given you, you will engage the Universal Law of Attraction with your positive feelings and definition.

Our thoughts become things which has been noted by many including a world renown teacher, thought leader, and philosopher Bob Proctor. By having the emotional feeling and by combining the feelings with our thoughts and take direct action on them they become things. If we keep our thoughts positive the determination and definite focus our feelings help provide our positive actions. We are adults, but when we look at babies, we can agree that their thoughts determine their actions and eventually they get their desired results.

Although we do not remember how we ourselves were as babies we can take time out and notice a baby's determined desire and focus to walk after crawling which is more proof of the Universal Law of Attraction. As for me I remember as far back as just before kindergarten and during those years you at least had to grasp some of the alphabet and some of your numerals. I had a severe stuttering problem and was very hyper. My desired outcome to learn the basics to attend kindergarten gave me the desire, the emotional feeling of success, and massive focus to compliment my success to enter kindergarten with the other kids.

Metaphorically you are the seedling that life is grooming to become a beautiful tree so be the mighty bamboo tree. It is puzzling to me of how it takes a bamboo seedling to be nurtured for the duration of 5 years to sprout from the ground and then grow to be a tree. What is so amazing is that not only in the 5th year of nurturing it breaks ground, but it can grow to the height of 90 feet in a month after it sprouts the ground! That is fascinating, but the lesson of the Chinese bamboo tree teaches us to have patience, perseverance, faith, and belief which are emotional actions and patterns in focus and the Law of attraction.

There are many effective ways to stay focused on your goals, and some work better than others, but the story behind the growth of the bamboo tree reminds us to stay confident and have faith while on the desired path of our focus. I personally love to meditate before I work or study to increase my awareness and focus. This allows for me to be consciously aware of my positive thoughts, ideas, and actions and required focus. This structured system that works for me and others allows the Universal Law of Attraction to do its work in mine and others lives.

In my imagination, I also love to envision the successful completion of my goal. I believe that what your mind can reveal too you is a vision of what you can have in your present reality. I also like to write my goals down often on paper to draw thoughts upon my actions. The goals I write down help to complete my days, weeks, and moths accordingly and are not like a New Year's resolution where I would begin making goals and in a matter of weeks or months forget the goals and blame my reason on the circumstances of life.

I love to envision my goals almost daily in the present tense of them being completed in the mornings and before I sleep. In not so great and in great circumstances this system worked for me and others never failing. Try my system for 30 days. Be the judge of how this structured system works in your life for the betterment of all your involvements.

Chapter 4

Focus and attraction are 2 very interesting words with meaning, and both words harmonize with

each other. To attract too you the successes or things that you want requires you to adjust your

beliefs and your focus on the things that you want. When you adjust your focus, you are engaging in attuning your mindset and vision for goal success without the negative shadows from doubt, fear, or worry. You will notice how you begin to attract those things of success that you want to yourself, but in keeping them you will find that you must have positive physical and mental focus on those things or scenarios that have positively affected your newly enhanced focused senses to them.

The laws of focus and the law of attraction will always be active in our lives and have been in the lives of human existence since the beginning of all ages and society's. It is as easy as waking and going to the bathroom in the morning to brush your teeth with certainty of a brighter and healthier smile as it is to engage in both focus and the law of attraction. Just think how when a baby crawls and tries to walk but falls. The baby's focus attracts to him/her what it wants which is to walk, and then actions of the baby working with desired focus and universal laws the walking becomes running!

As we lived to grow to become older individuals blossoming out from the baby stage, we began to allow our perfect imperfections to cause us to make ignorant mistakes, and we began to allow doubts, fears, and worries to take president in our minds during moments like our teenage years, young adult years, and parenting years. My meaning of having ignorance is to be in a conscious state of not knowing the truth, seeing the truth as an illusion or an obstacle to be learned. Although our minds work perfectly in the right of our bodies, but without conscious focus from us, they can sometimes help to create the perfect quiet stealth like storm welcoming the mental imperfections doubts, fears, or worries. Our bodies and conscious minds give us focus and the law of attraction, together both calibrating as a team working as gifts from God and the Universe in our best interest.

Do not complain or focus on the things that you do not want to have or see happening or happen in a manner that you cannot change a plan for or discern the path too. As the serenity prayer states:

God grant me the serenity to accept the things I cannot "change" ...   Stay in a positive state of belief and maintain your mental ability to focus and allow the law of focus and the law of attraction to work in your life for you. There may be some delay when you focus on the stars, but at least you will land on the moon, and during the delay the law of attraction will not fail you promising to reset the course and successfully your goal.

In my younger years I did not know God, the universe, understand the law of focus, or the law of attraction. I often attracted to me and focused on that which I did not like or want unwilling and unintendedly by negative thoughts, actions, and complaints. The result was an accumulation of stress which had resulted in me having a TBI or traumatic brain injury in my early 20's. To me the event was a lesson and a blessing of love to be understood, trusted in, and to truly understand and feel the love god and the universe had for me.

I understand my past event to be a lesson of love from god, the universe, and began to trust in them and understand more of nature and natural abundance. The laws of focus and attraction became clear to my attention more and more, and I began to take notice to them and study them. Each morning I start the day with writing a gratitude list and I love how it gives me focus to the positive aspects of my daily life. Writing my gratitude list each morning helps me to start seeing all the salty moments in my past and present life as sweet moments, giving me the appropriated positive attitude needed for each day before I begin to process my day ahead.

Past moments have a way of getting our attention to re-adjusting our focus. Many lessons learned along our path are needed to be presented too and conquered by us for us to use and understand our strengths, and to give us the nudge we need to decide and identify with our feelings and situation. Many things present themselves for us to know and understand our inner yearning and desire, to trust and believe God and the universe. God, the universe, and the laws of nature or also known as the universal laws will aid us in going from a lack mindset to a prosperity mindset.

When we learn to let go of the problems we face daily, be it emotionally, financially, or physically and learn to allow them to manifest in thought form as solutions. Our minds are simply physical computers in the flesh. I am not saying that we are part robots, although there are some people with prosthetic arms, I am saying that we can update our minds like the computer updates its data base and systems. I believe that our minds are like computers by the way we learn, store, and process things.

Nor our minds or computers stop to a complete silence of doing absolutely nothing, thinking unconsciously or according to programming when sleeping. During R.E.M. sleep our subconscious part of our mind is still running so we cannot simply click a switch and turn it off. Also, unlike computers, our mind has vivid dreams like that of a movie playing as we lay still in our slumber. Likewise, when a computer is being turned on, we humans also have a wake time. Our wake time is innate within our minds, or can be due to an alarm clock, whereas computers use built in clock computing system.

Like computers we learn things by researching and gathering information. Computers have built in search engines to gather information and as we live life, we humans gather the needed information to thrive and love life. Think about human evolution which is the process that lead to the emergence of anatomically modern humans or homo sapiens. For thousands of years humankind has recorded its history either by structures, paintings, or books.

Natural laws convincing of the law of attraction and the law of focus are primary through human evolution and human history. Computers have not been around in existence for nearly as long but take the stage with a standing novation by simply storing vast quantities of information on hard drives, soft drives, or flash drives. My goal was to paint a beautiful picture that has a correlation between the human mind and computers in your mind which is a true ordeal in our daily lives. Addressing the correlation between the human mind and the computer in a respective proves to be both informative and beneficial to our future growth and existence.

Much of the human mind's information is given through generational teachings which is processed in our minds by hereditary means. Computer systems can research the akashic records or ancestry.com to gain an in-depth view of human conception forming from generational birth. Man, and computers are alike in many ways. Generational births, technology, and communication both aid to help expand our history as humankind.

We humans store images of our history in picture forms or visualizations in our minds. The computer stores most of its information in a hard drive, prone cyber-attacks or security breaches, but often saves the files in a safe place. This does not make the computer less effective, but more effective because it stores millions of bytes of data and holds files that the human mind cannot process or hold for the many changing years without a blemish. Just as the Universal Law of Attraction and the Law of Focus work together in harmony so does the human mind and computers.

Chapter 5

I have learned that it is easier to have and maintain your focus when you understand the Universal Law of Attraction. The Universal Law of Attraction states how you attract to you how you think and feel. The use of your thoughts and feelings are attractive to your goals and desires. The universal law of attraction also implies that you attract to you that which you who you are.

I love myself and spread love on social media outlets, on my nature walks, my work details, when writing my daily gratitude list, and my daily affairs. In all I do throughout the day, I do my best to come from a place of love when doing it and the universal law of attraction gives back to me love. The Universal Law of attraction gives the gift of attraction to you through your thoughts and feelings while you are wake and even in your sleep. The universal law of attraction is a law that proves how what you think and feel attracts to you what and how you think and feel which also creates the atmosphere see and resonate with around you.

I am positive that you have a conscious understanding of what your thoughts and your feelings are towards a person or entity that is attracted to you. It does not matter if you never went to college, have written a book, nailed an awesome career job, or have focused on maintaining millions of dollars. In this age of information there is no excuse for anyone to lack knowledge if they seek for knowledge that is prudent to their affairs. Anyone who seeks knowledge engages in obtaining power by directing their mind to focus.

In this age of information, we have the use of technology and have the use of our natural instincts our thoughts and feelings. Keeping these qualities in mind, we come to know that the use of focus and the Universal Law of Attraction are both in play together in our lives as we grow in our lives.

We know that having the technology, the natural law of focus, and the universal law of attraction heighten our daily relationships and deliver to us our desired results. In this age of information and the prior ages we have always been co-creators of our own universe.

We can consider succeeding in school, going to college, and the meaning behind making a certain grade or having to have maintained a certain grade or GPA (grade point average) in school, and college a societal norm. We can also consider them to be triumphs as we grow with our focus and allow the universal law of attraction to gives us what we attract or focus on.   When you focus on what you want, think, feel and are you attract to you more of what you want, think, feel, and are. Both the natural law of focus and the universal law of attraction are Masters of Design.

I would like for you to see that your free will to focus and the steadfast movement of the Universal Law of Attraction applies to all areas of our human day to day lifestyles. Although we are in the age of information and the use of technology makes socializing more widespread by way of internet connection, the law of focus and the law of the universal law of attraction are 2 natural laws that will always be in human nature. It is very important that you continue to keep your thoughts, feelings, and actions positive even during the moments in life that you feel stressed and overwhelmed. Some moments are intense in feelings such as heartbreaks, funerals, and weddings, but your good health and wealth is respective of your positive well-being.

Please remember that whether you are religious or spiritual that the Universal law of Attraction is always at work in your favor. When the universal law of attraction is combined with focus it will attract to you any vibration that you think and feel. Please keep your feelings and thoughts positive and enjoy loving in a visual the life you focus on. Always remember that what we focus on grows and our thoughts and feelings are our greatest most powerful creators during each human evolution age.

"The light of the body is in the eye;

if thine eye be single, thy whole body shall be full of light.

Mattew 6:22

The natural law of focus is a natural\universal law of importance that leads you to understanding the universal law of attraction and how to better attract with the universal law of attraction by use of the natural law of focus. To have a better understanding of the universal law of attraction, it is pertinent for us to first learn and understand the universal law of focus and this book entails the steps of focusing. This law tells us how our attention must always be focused on our goals, vision, and our purpose. When you use intentional focus you also control your thoughts, feelings and actions.

The more positively focused that you are in obtaining your goals the more that positive attractions will become present to you. The universal law of attraction will always match you and your success of the goal you seek as it will also bring you to become more positively focused with the energy you vibrate with while focusing in the completion of success. To focus with intent requires self-discipline. Self-discipline is a key factor in focus and is also one of the most important factors in focus.

Self-discipline requires belief in yourself that thrives of the will to succeed. Self-discipline requires you to roll with the punches in life, but to not give into any of the pressures. Another great thing about self-discipline is that it requires you to get busy on reaching your goals. Your actions will cause intention which will make it easier for you to master the art of acting as if your wish is fulfilled, and for the universal law of attraction to deliver to you your wish fulfilled.

Self-discipline also requires you to maintain your focus and a huge amount of faith, belief, and hope.

"None of us knows what might happen even the next minute, yet still we go forward. Because we trust. Because we have Faith." — Paulo Coelho

Chapter 6

Let nothing dim the light that shines from within.

Maya Angelou.

Use the magnetic approaches that will dramatically increase your focus, which will positively engage the law of attraction, and allow your light to shine brighter than ever before. Focusing and the engagement of the universal law of attraction will entice begin to follow the path of least resistance. The path of least resistance is the physical and the mental starting path which you will follow by your intuitive guidance system or God sense mind.

Your intuitive guidance system will trust and follow the peaceful harmony of the path of least resistance while you move forward focusing on your goals. I found the path of least resistance when I began to meditate more and listen and trust my intuition softly spoken words more. There is a song by instrumentalist, singer, actor Jimmy Cliff titled I Can See Clearly Now. In the song he states how he can see clearly now that the rain is gone referring to himself and the clearing of his mind to focus.

He sings about how he can see all obstacles in his way. He was telling a story how he had regained his focus allowing him to see and follow the path of least resistance. The universal law of attract gave Jimmy Cliff what he had been focusing on. Jimmy Cliff's vision became clear and the path of least resistance had appeared for him.

Focus combined with the universal law of attraction lead me down the path of least resistance of financial freedom. I knew that payday loans, college loans, and hospital bills was not my destiny. Finishing college was a goal of mine and writing books was a passion. I began to focus on my goals of becoming a success in all that I was led to do and become.

What seemed like resistance to me at first was God and the universe's way of giving me gratitude for all my hard work and dedication. My focus and the universal law of attraction became magnetic, bringing me to seek the opportunity down the path of least resistance. My story is proof that you are both a lesson and a blessing. I have learned that we shape our own success allowing the natural and universal laws that exist to prevail.

Chapter 7

I ask myself often about whether I am in integrity with myself and my feelings. I have learned

that by me consciously focusing on the feel-good thoughts I have, that they also bring to me a feel-

good feeling. My reality began to change the moment more of my focus began to grow with where

my integrity had lied. We all have a goal in common and that goal is a desire to be more in

alignment with ourselves and the love energy.

We all were born in the love energy and will return to a higher understanding of the love energy

after we become one with our human deaths. Focusing builds character and a positive self-image.

What you actively focus on becomes what you attract more of too you in accordance with the universal law of attraction. Stay focused on the positive aspects of problems and solutions to support and will begin to attract to you more positive problems and solutions.

Focus on things like good health, prosperity, or wealth. Focus on not being poor to attract to you a rich and vibrant life. Always believe in yourself. Believe in yourself more than those who choose to not believe in you or your goals.

Focus on finding and nurturing your unique gifts and begin attracting to you more abundance! Success is when you learn from your failures so by finding and nurturing your gifts you are in a vortex of learning successes at a rapid rate. Both harmony and balance are always positive in our nature just as success and good health. Abundance and success are our nature as we are one with god and the universe.

Poverty is a disease and we are not sick. When we focus on sickness, we attract to us more life episodes of sickness. When we focus on good health and wealth, we attract to us a life of good health and wealth. Likewise, when we focus on the things we deem as poverty we attract to us the things we deem as poverty.

Poverty lies in the lack mindset with all negative energetic things. We tend to associate good things with wealth and riches. We associate bad things with poverty, a lack mindset, or negative things. Many things including a lack mindset does not mean poverty. Poverty is a disease made to conquer and control our minds and having a lack mindset only aids the lesser of abundant thinking and having prosperity in our lives.

Prosperity gives you the right to think about thoughts that manifest into wealth, good health, and more prosperity as your alignment to the prosperity frequency increases and the law of attraction always gives to you the frequency you match. People with a prosperity mindset invite happiness into their lives. They do this on a constant basis by giving, feeling, and showing gratitude for all things big and small. People with a growth mindset or live in a steady conscious awareness of prosperity always think of ideas to be the solution to their and other's problems.

This is different among people with a lack mindset because they consistently think of things to gossip about adding problems to their initial problem. People with a lack mindset also tend to focus on things that are stressful to them such as their spiral of health issues and their constant complaining of everyday living bills. People with a lack mindset attract to them more things of problems, stress, and lack. In today's world there are millions of individuals that live in the global society who choose to focus on news media outlets which nurture lack over prosperity.

I have learned to notice how my thoughts, feelings, and habits were helping me to condition and stabilize a prosperity mindset and to not groom for myself a lack mindset. Living a stressful, but happily settled life, that went from week to week living and making a paycheck only to pay bills each week was not in my focus. When I began to understand more of myself, I knew that chasing one job just to afford the bills that were in my current reality only to exchange the less than $20,000 annually paying job for another job that does the same is of the lack mindset. I have learned much about my thoughts, actions, and reactions by growing from a lack mindset to a prosperity mindset.

To grow to a prosperity mindset from a lack mindset you need to understand that you are rich. I know that the comment immediately made many readers suddenly think about their bank account, particularly their savings account, and the cause and effects done to their bank account from their living lifestyle. To be rich means that you realize that you create happiness for yourself and for those around you. To be rich and feel the richness inside you resonates with the law of attraction, and the law of attraction brings to you more riches because that is the vibration that the law had resonated with.

When you have a focus on your thoughts, feelings, and actions concerning riches god and the universe will bring to you your wish of riches fulfilled. The more you have faith and belief in yourself adds to the fact that you have the power to attract to you and create what you desire in life. This is a model of the prosperity consciousness which enhances the energy that your attitude and self-image will reflect. Your attitude will always be an indication of your altitude in your growing prosperity consciousness.

Focus on only the things that you want to manifest in your life and the positive focus that you give will polish brightly all aspects of your world. Always allow your thoughts, feelings, and actions to respectfully respond positively on the goals you choose to focus on. Abraham Hicks stated "Think the thought until you believe it, and once you believe it, it is. Bob Proctor even voiced his opinion on how your thoughts become things as he stated," Thoughts become things. If you see it in your mind, you will hold it in your hand."

What makes things even more interesting is when you act on the universal law of attraction while staying in alignment with the universal law of focus. The universal law of focus specifies that we move toward what we focus on, just as your thoughts create actions, your thoughts create the actions from what you choose to focus on. Keep your thoughts and actions positive.